# SING LOVE 101
## (Poems)

## Bill F. Ndi

**Langaa Research & Publishing CIG**
*Mankon, Bamenda*

*Publisher:*

*Langaa* RPCIG
Langaa *Research & Publishing Common Initiative Group*
P.O. Box 902 Mankon
Bamenda
North West Region
Cameroon
Langaagrp@gmail.com
www.langaa-rpcig.net


Distributed outside N. America by African Books Collective
orders@africanbookscollective.com
www.africanbookcollective.com


Distributed in N. America by Michigan State University Press
msupress@msu.edu
www.msupress.msu.edu


*ISBN: 9956-579-04-1*

DISCLAIMER
All views expressed in this publication are those of the author
and do not necessarily reflect the views of Langaa RPCIG.

# DEDICATION

To all those who love unconditionally and have known happiness in their love lives. It is also dedicated to all those who have hit the rocks in their love lives with the sole purpose that the latter remember the worst thing about a fall is not the fall in itself but the inability to sit up or get up after one hits the rocks and falls in the cracks of love. LG= Love's Good! Keep Loving!

# Table of Content

Author's Note.................................................... vii

Preface........................................................ ix

The Musical Hand............................................. 1

Garden in the Heart.......................................... 3

Nostalgia..................................................... 3

To Me......................................................... 4

Love.......................................................... 5

Heart Beats................................................... 6

Soluej (Parts)................................................ 6

Lovers' Prayer................................................ 7

Val (*Veracious, Admirable, Lovable*)....................... 8

Letter to C................................................... 9

My Love above All............................................ 9

My Bond...................................................... 10

My Love in the Moon.......................................... 12

My Calm Spring............................................... 13

Sweet Honey.................................................. 14

A Bold Step.................................................. 14

Invitation................................................... 15

The Flight................................................... 16

Not Over My Belle............................................ 17

A Dream for U J.............................................. 18

Dreams Are Dreams............................................ 18

Love Unrequited.............................................. 19

The Jolt..................................................... 19

A Special Find............................................... 20

Epigrams 1................................................... 20

Epigrams 2................................................... 21

Epigrams 21.................................................. 21

Epigrams 35.................................................. 21

Epigrams 64.................................................. 22

Epigrams 78.................................................. 22

Epigrams 82......................................................... 23
Epigrams 84......................................................... 23
My Watch and I..................................................... 23
Thorns of Love..................................................... 24
Thorny Bush Love................................................. 25
Thicket Dance...................................................... 25
Broken Seeking Heart............................................ 26
Poem for Migrants................................................ 26
Prickling Thorn.................................................... 27
Heartbeat in a Tomb.............................................. 27
To The Altar to Be Altered..................................... 28
The Death of Darling............................................. 28
Forty Years After, No Honey................................... 30
The Pursuit......................................................... 31
Questions for Union.............................................. 32
The Flash of Beauty.............................................. 33
Weak Strength!.................................................... 34
The Infidel Spouse............................................... 35
All Apostles?...................................................... 36
Lady Z.............................................................. 37
Platter of Abuse.................................................. 39
Yellow Leaf Forever.............................................. 40
Poisonous Heart.................................................. 41
K Joiner............................................................ 41
The Walls of My Love............................................ 42
The Lion and Attraction......................................... 42
Tears for Peace and Love........................................ 43
Dulcet.............................................................. 44
The Longing........................................................ 44
Love Sake.......................................................... 45
276/286............................................................ 46
Love Hope.......................................................... 47
Strange............................................................. 47
Flower Pot Music................................................. 49

iv

Fill Thy Measure Full.................................... 50

Zero!................................................ 51

Love by the Right Dose............................... 51

We'll Fly............................................ 52

Voice to My Words................................... 53

Love Professor Screwed.............................. 54

Sky Kissing Earth.................................... 54

Love You Forever.................................... 55

Hi Stranger! Miss You!............................... 56

Demon in the Attic.................................. 57

Smells of Death..................................... 57

Love in Pitch Darkness............................... 58

Treason Felon....................................... 58

The Face of Beauty.................................. 59

She Went To School.................................. 60

Some Desires........................................ 61

Tamara.............................................. 62

How Far To Go?..................................... 63

Lullaby for Love.................................... 63

Before The Courts................................... 64

Our Separate Ways.................................. 64

The Second Christening.............................. 65

Walk the Walk...................................... 65

Run For Love........................................ 66

Seeing On 20th, Meeting On 21st...................... 68

Strong Rock Solid Love.............................. 69

Sheila Is All........................................ 70

Our Growing Love................................... 71

What D.... Does!.................................... 72

The Sound Of Reality................................ 72

To You I Sing....................................... 73

I Refuse............................................. 74

Give the World...................................... 75

Dreams Die Not..................................... 76

Two Months After.................................................... 76
That We Won't Take................................................. 78
Blurred Vision........................................................ 79

Praise for these Poems........................................... 81

# Author's Note

Love and compassion, Loss and gain, grief and bliss, incorruptibility and knowledge, society and politics, successes and failures, haps and *Mishaps*... leave none unaffected safe one whose heart has fossilised. Writing poetry over the ages has been and still is a means of expressing those deep innermost feelings that transcend human emotions. Cf. Preface of *Mishaps and Other Poems*.

In this volume it is more about LOVE in all its ramifications as well as all the emotions that true love and disappointed love would arouse. Having had experience of true love as well as disappointment in love, it was worth I shared some of these very intrinsically strong personal feelings and experiences so the poet's words do not become mere words to be thrown left and right but those to be lived personally and shared with all those we love, are in love with and/or those with whom we have fallen out of love. What is worth doing than having to share this spontaneous overflow of powerful feelings? I so do with stark simplicity as LOVE, per se, is simple to live were all to stop complicating it for themselves. It is in simplicity that love finds its worth and weight in my verse, *Sing Love 101*. The poems are positive, romantic, tragic and easy to digest like any basic 100 level college course or introductory course any, who is interested in being initiated to the stakes of love, would never want to skip.

*Bill F NDI*

# Preface

It is often said that love, both sacrosanct and sacrilegious, is the only true subject of the lyric poem, and nothing better justifies this claim than the fabulous poems in this collection. Bill Ndi in his usual style hurls himself through various emotional dispositions from sadness to exhilaration, from erotic through platonic to filial, representing the various facets of love's expression for even at its most piercing; love remains a universal experience of the human soul. These poems contribute significantly in humanizing Ndi who is well known for his politically caustic poems, and shows that even a committed poet can still leave his house on fire to chase a mole rat fleeing from its flames. The 101 poems in this stunning collection are noted for their lushness of language and simplicity of style as they explore a wide range of emotions while embodying the fearless passion and spirited wit of a poet to whom like Pablo Neruda, words are fun. As you mingle effortlessly through the pages, you will discover that this collection bears the best poetry for new love or old love; requited or unrequited love; fulfilled or unfulfilled love; in fact, any love for as is underscored in the concluding verse of the "The Musical Hand," "Loving infinitely as we do is nothing but wisdom for nothing other than wisdom is infinite!". Why not make this a Veracious Admirable Loveable Valentine present.

**Festus Fru Ndeh, Associate Professor of Postcolonial and Theoretical Literatures, Troy University, USA.**

# The Musical Hand

Of you thinking still
                                    Still and calm
                    At night
                To a solitary chamber
            Abandoned,
Only the clock's music
Company kept
And would none told me
Of the passing time
Nor of that to come
For the long awaited one has come
And we have to dance to the rhythm
                Of our love
                        Set by the ticking clock
                                            I sat
                                        I looked
                                                And

was dazed

By this clock's

            Hands

                    Like destiny's

                    And like in a race

                    Running

            To drowninG

1

The rest Of humanity

To the gravE

Fading out their joyS of the old

Reminding them the foretold

                                        Sorrows
                                        Of the morrows
                        But for me
But for my lovely love, my darling
With whom I am dazed
Not with astonishment
By amazement
Dazzled
For these hands
Draws us
Closer and closer
And to bliss closer
Justifying our reason
To joyously dance all round every season
And to this rhythm
Of the ticking clock
Playing lovers' desire
With its regularity in rhythm!
With a challenge from the second hand to any
To show the world him/she
That would theirs for temporised
Not my love, not me
For we love
And forever will LOVE
And in our gaze will not see
Mr. Taim, a passer-by

Pass by!
Loving infinitely as we do is nothing but wisdom for nothing
other than wisdom is infinite!


## Garden in the Heart

In my heart a garden blooms
With roses and just no rooms
In sight for a heart that's not pure
Attempt not to my garden lure
For sinuousness she knows not
But with labyrinth fraught
To make rotten hearts manure
To feed my rose fresh for sure
So, one can plug, smell and kiss her
As mine needs one with such in her.


## Nostalgia

On my bed in sleepless ennui
Rolling round and round
My thoughts are turned unto that one Lady
On whose laps I slept warm and sound
And these thoughts rolling my eyes
Goad my expectations to seeing this belle
Yet, all that's left is none but the stony
Source of my tears' Spring
Letting the tears roll down my cheeks
Whenever I roll the balls of these Eyes
In the way of my bony
Lass!!

By Gwad!!
Take away my food
Take away my drink
Take away my peace
And give me no sleep
Nor rest
But give me her
And I will show you
That all I lost I found
She is Food
Drink
Sleep
Peace
And rest
And this is the Lady I, like everyone, for
Long Longed for !!

## TO ME

I doubt if there is need being lonely
For you know one can never tell
What is hidden in the heart of a black dark night
Nor behind the back of a bright sunny day.

How I wish you could be seen!
Oh! Happiness shall never end
For the sweetest are the most dear
And in the vast space, scattered they're.

To trace my steps, I very much long for,
If I could know you really Love, how happy?
Nevertheless, you would have longed as I do.

But, when shall this reciprocity come?

Where the truth lies, few people know.
And to search very few take the pains
For none amongst the few come by it;
They capitulate with a sunken face.

Me, seeing the truth by you,
I don't think I would as those
From the quest, carry a sunken face
For I my happiness see reflecting on your face.


## LOVE

Whether it exists or not
Depends on the personalities
Who perform the act;
Actors best know
Their position in the affair.

Love can be made
Lovable if the bitterness
Is forgone for the sweetness!
Nevertheless, the consequences
Forgone can be
Just good as well as *bad*…..
But all is love
The making.

# HEART BEATS

Together, two hearts,
Brought, than with
Passion consume fruits
Of Mother Nature,
These two with awe
Uphold staring
As if pricked by some strange sting
And would not embrace
And digest the crumbs
     Of sentiments
Ridding them of sediments
With Patience's
Abject prescience
To turn miraculous,
Consummation Magnanimous....
Chanted songs by the world
Did traverse the tympanum and no word
         Stored;

Yet, savoured
Every hiss as would eyes
      On lakeside Roses.


## Søluej (parts)

Your absence, I see rise like fever
Provoked by the venomous purple serpent
That swallowed and kept you in her bowel;
When it trailed off, its vertebrae squeaking,
All left of this hoping
Wan seeing you concealed

And in a dark compartment sealed;
Your store,
Was hearts' sore….
Still I hope for distance
I know dead for hearts,
Static ones with psyche obliterating
A notion so strange to a 'cosm;
And madder still in love,
I burn like a stove….


## LOVERS' PRAYER

Mauryn,
The screen
Through which I see
The flowery
Nature nurture
To feast my lens
At heart
In sleepless dreams
With your colour
Dregless
Like penguin's fidelity
In front of which I bow
To make you my ego;
You blossom
Like moorland greenery
And being equine I can't be dreary;

Nights up
In insomnia
A thought rings

Church bell-like
Telling the sleeping laity
To sit up,
Decide their faith,
Gluing to too faith
For faith is theirs
And devotedly I am yours!

Mauryn,
Willing to do this,
In my sleeplessness
I would I see God;
Let him know my heart I got
Into your thoracic cage
Out of my left rib framed,
Drench your mind's eyes
With my love for you;
Urgeless to sever
The bond of our tie
As I wish blindness our forte,
Blindness to the infidels' world
You are mine in mind.

## VAL (*Veracious, Admirable, Lovable*)

Would my pens dry up
Every lake, ocean, river, sea and stream
To pen a poem,
One for missing you
The story is long for these short pens…

# LETTER TO C

The heart's needs
Warrant skids
And not skits
At a glance
Doubts rushed to the grave
Challenging the grave
That I was, once.
I took you by the hand
And those behind whom I ran
Will they snatch me from you
To hear me say, I el oh vee ee love U,
For my heart tells me you are mine
And I yours, must carry you in mind.


# MY LOVE ABOVE ALL

When I listen to my heart beat
Thy sweet melodious music I hear hit
And I tell no tales
For I am no storyteller
But a desert traveller
Who wandered round Paris
With just no hopes finding an oasis
But mirages
And bobbed up that eve of my new age
Across one revealing
Every cloud's silver lining
With me pushed to diving
In
And would fish I became

By Rachael's frame
To dwell well
In her well
My heart, My love
That makes forget the dose
Of ennui inhabiting all those
Seeking great names
Seeking great political offices
Seeking material wealth
Seeking everything earthly great.

Rachael my heart
Rachael my love
Rachael my passion
Rachael my vision
Of thee I make my dream
And with thee in a strong team
For our love is above everything earthly great
And thou art my R…. the greatest of the great
        We shall sing down the street
        Hand in hand for thou art so sweet…!

                Paris, 08/28/1998. 14:35:21.


## MY BOND

R… Queen of Hearts
Crowned King, King of cats!

R…., the King shall never leave thee cuts
And never shall he but thee buts!

R… my love I found
My life shall by thee be bound!

Rachael my love I love
Our living together shall be enough!

Rachael my love I think of
Thy love has made me tough!

Rachael the heart beating in me
Drives in me one desire, "Rachael I wish to see."

Rachael my love for whom I crave
My life is and shall be with thee till the grave!

Rachael I love till my grave,
Thine is the one love to make me grave!

Rachael my love with whom I am serious
My love with thine shall drive the world jealous!

Rachael my love for thee I craze
Our love is our grace!

And gracefully finding the quiet of loving,
Of it we must make a keeping!

# MY LOVE IN THE MOON

Lifting my head to the sky
I had but one desire
Seeing the big bright
Moon reflecting that high
My calm love
No wonder
I would I fly
To embrace her
To whisper to her
My love for her
Is reflected

And sitting up, up
In the moon
Reflecting her…
Bright
Bride
Igniting the flame
That burns for bells
To toll
Announcing journey time
Honeymoon
Journey time.

Love, we must….
Make this journey to the moon
Where there is sweet, sweet honey
Awaiting us to feast for life
As Husband                    and                    wife

# MY CALM SPRING

                    Come, come stay
For you are my muse
Come inhabit me this way!
If you don't I'll come
Come make you my fuse
And with no fuss transport electricity
Transforming all into light
Generating heat in cold Winter
                    Cold in hot, hot summer.

Thou maketh the man grow
Thou maketh my pen flow
Through the river bed, our heart
To inundate sheets with LOVE
Showing the world now love
Is the possiblest impossibility
At first sight
And must never be taken light
As thou reflect thy starry light
On the path of our true love
Intimating me to stand above
The carnal wish and think of just one thing

My Calm Spring!

I turned round and round questing the bloom of a flowery
garden with none till my lovely spring with her refreshing
water quenched my thirst and with her light and calm showed
up like a swallow from a distance for me to decide same
instance to follow her to where like a river I shall take my rise
by her side.

# Sweet Honey

Sweet,
Sweet,
Sweet
Honey
Bee u tee
When thou sting
None can sing
With the pain
None can disdain
Thee and thy praise
And only the insane
Can rise to race
Being one in admiration for U I dance
Thy sweet, sweet dance...!
Especially with thee by me
On my knee
I glory
And with joy
Enjoy
       Thee bee u tee,
Thy labour, honey!

# A Bold Step

Onward truest lovers
In the fields of love
Treading
Needn't stagger
For such is reserved for beggars
For love begging

And I neither am timid
Nor you frigid
For all it takes is a bold step
And up we'll find the help
True lovers desire: courage and above
All, like Jove
King and Queen crowned
For we this step made
And with true love shall be paid
All our span….!


## INVITATION

Each time I look at a diary
The lines spreading plane I see
With no inscription inviting me….
No, my pen to place his inky
Lips as I would mine on my love's
For the exchange of lovely kisses
So does my pen
So am I of pain
Relieved
Seeing my pen is letting flow
The lovely ink not revealing
His love for the paper
But mine for my love
Whose charms leave no fel-
Low indifferent
Safe he that fell
Low and became different!

As my heart beats rise

So do I like dough rise
Each day and it suffices, rice
Or none I know the price
For this love
Is bone
Strong
And strong
I am in love


## The Flight

With your noble-like flight to Grenoble
Gracefully colourful
My bee u tea full
Butterfly
My heart's eye
On thee humbly riveted
As you bring home nothing noble
But this plight
And this heart's
D
  O
    W
      N
Heavily
  And tinted.

# Not Over My Belle

I often blamed people for being thieves
Yet, I blame not she who from me all blessings receives
For she has stolen my Heart
And I feel the warmth of a hearth!
Valentine if you truly are a saint
Then, in life you must not have had a taint
And I would you convince the world you truly are patron
Over my Belle whose love like steel is strong
Like water is pure
Like medicine is a cure
Like a ruler is straight
Like believe is faith
Like song is soft
Like farmland is a croft
I can go on and on yet, I must end
But your saintliness wouldn't make me bend
For in my Belle, the thief,
She stole a heart that soared above the cliff
For Love and her way,
Made him sway.
Valentine could you have been a thief and a saint,
Or could you have infringed the law never to be a saint?
Sure? I am not. For you are not my belle!
And if you were all would have tolled the bell
Whose soft music our ears would have caressed
Leaving me a-dancing like the possessed.

# A DREAM FOR U J...!

I have a dream
For U my love
A dream
For U and me
A unique nation
The one and endless ocean
So calm
To soothe like balm
In which together we must...
Must swim
For she with her crystal clear
Waters
Mirroring the bluest of skies
Is named Joy Infinite!
Embrace the courage and let me dive
And even sink
To give meaning to life
And you, I bet, with ecstasy will sing...!


# DREAMS ARE DREAMS

My dream, to meet love
My dream, to love the love
                              I meet
My dream, to break the shell of solitude
Through the endless river of Lovitude
Through me flowing...!

There it rebounds:
Fate...?

18

Fight or fight not?

The more I love
My love
The more
In my mirror
I meet aloneness
And yes…!
No terrestrial
Nor celestial
Mare would stop me,
Stop me
From loving my love

                                        KIS…!


## LOVE UNREQUITED

Both hand and heart I gave
                              You
Hand you strapped 'n with heart played;
Fun, 'twas for you!
And with mourning I'm paid!


## THE JOLT

I would the stabbing from other quarters came!
I would have cried out your name!
But, from you coming, I laugh:
My passion only, LOVE
Kills me!

# A SPECIAL FIND

Nothing on earth matches finding
True love and sincerely loving!
Having found one true love, would she
Realised this sincerity from the profundity
Generating
Strength to unveiling
She remains that very special one
To take all my care and attention:
Beauty reincarnated,
Love born to the human world
Standing for care
And my bands playing for her
To savour the sweetness of the drumbeats of a heart
When at lonely nights thoughts of her drum a spark
Reflecting none but her B.U.T....!


# Epigrams 1

If one told thee
In love there was 'rithmetic,
With one word, retort:
LIE!
Supply
Her with emotion
If she seeks thine opinion
'Cause She springs from the Heart
never from the head!

# Epigrams 2

Nice guy
Show thy love to any
And as they back reciprocity
Welcome another....
But if all negate,
Show them, hitchless is
Life without them
And if any, imagination
In the self will defy that!

# Epigrams 21

Gloom is seen
When the cosmos gleam
Bleak with dearth knocking at doors
For prostitute love to sneak in through
windows
Leaving humour alone
To retort foundation,
Supporting roots
To stabilising
The set crumbling…!

# Epigrams 35

When you reciprocate love
Loving truly for even just one minute
None would ever mind
Asking you if you harboured thoughts

At all; the love would forever last
And all shall forever
Love, care
And cherish ya
The winner…!


## Epigrams 64

When I heard a woman
Shout, shouting at a man:
"There are men out there,
Men out there to love me
Men out there to cherish me
And those to treat me like a queen…
Bla…! Bla…! Bla…!"
Silently, I told myself:
"Not until they taste of the quinine
You are, you will never see how loved
'N cherished you are and have been by a King!"


## Epigrams 78

A person can trick another
Tricking them into a relationship
And taking them far
Far, far away from all relatives
With dreams of keeping them submissive
But can't trick themselves,
Tricking themselves to loving
Even when the tricked is unfailing
In their unconditional love for the trickster…

# Epigrams 82

Feeling pity
And not Love
For another human being
Is born of ignorance:
Fooling oneself of being
Better than a fellow
Traveller, one in this journey towards the grave
But loving them for being human
Is born of the cognizance
Of the oneness of humanity

# Epigrams 84

When striving for things better
As would a dove,
Never choose money & power
                                    Over
Love
              And              Peace
And voice nothing in anger
For that which is of anger
Born is never sweet but always bitter

# My Watch and I

My watch on my wrist stuck
As if to feel my pulse
Late last night my heart struck
By her to caress impulse

Did rise, kiss, laugh and stroke her.

I would not her grip she released
For the grip with great joy fills me
If this she does none would be pleased
'Coz my bonnet will hold a bee
Stopping my heart ticking for her

So, separate me not from my watch
She set my heart to start racing
I shall race till the race will hatch
A chick with the second ticking
Such bliss to be with and match with her.

## Thorns of Love

At the campaign we only saw a picture
We'd better walk him in to see the feature
His picture was spotless and stainless
So we hopped and danced for his holiness

Falling in love blinds to the fact
Tiny little hair can kill the pact
When it's grown big pulling its weight like thorn
In the flesh of love heavier than a ton

Copy such love not, keep eyes wide open
Keeping away all foul fowls in pen
Conditions by the tons
For true love make their thorns

At close range the hairy face freckles show

Stainlessness and spotlessness were pre-show
Forced unto us for love of near reality
When for real all other is indeed reality


## Thorny Bush Love

If I fell in a thorny bush
Bush I would have blamed
For being legged lame
In a thorn of love I fall, shush!
For Bush like nature is wild
Where love from you should be mild
Not Chenneying a friend as a game
And not in a duel for a dame.


## Thicket Dance

In the thicket of harmful thorns
Harmlessly danced would-be newborn
At birth, the thicket of thorns cleared
With just a few with efforts geared
To see they of their harmfulness use
Make of the vale of rose bright abuse;
Vale in which newborn will be buried
Vale that the masked crime warheads carried
With their veil of charity lords
Barricaded behind stone forts
Stone forts blood baths clean
Traces to redeem
These mean lords
Backing chords,

Those which will tune
A festive June
Music has never known
Before birth of unknown

## Broken Seeking Heart

Like heat in a snowy weather
Things could never be any better
For a heart full of love
By thorn pricked and turned off
For the snow no heat needs
Like a broken heart needs
The icy cold breeze for refreshment
Of a seeking heart questing movement
Towards a warm heart in cold
Longing never to grow old.

## Poem for Migrants

The world we do go round
In search of a butt that's round
One we do find but hard
To convince the bard
The bard a she won't see
We have for the world beauty
Taken her and for cognizance
She would the priest's reconnaissance
Needless for unconditional love
That would this world feed more than enough
And 'coz we maintain and slave

What was the best we then gave
We still and will think the world round
Will go around any butt round
Buxom round butt gelatine
That's the heart's Clementine
Love, take it or not
Let me crack the nut
I will love and love her round butt
And of her I will dream and dream love rut.


## Prickling Thorn

Plunging in the well hopes nursed!
Then flames from hell our lives cursed
Sending us hell bound far from our dreams
Being swept away by the flooding streams
With the streams receding hopes went
And in this overflow we wend
With its prickling thorns
In our world this war torn.


## Heartbeat in a Tomb

I have lost a loved one
The one I love has just been entomb
And on my knees I go down this tomb
And with my ears on it, I scan,
And guess what I do hear
Just nothing to bring fear;
I hear a heartbeat
A heart that with love beat

Saying true love knows no end
When in tombs bodies mark their end.


## To the Altar to Be Altered

Human unconsciousness volumes speaks
When the dark secret its apogee peaks
Then the darkness lights up in the dark
And past imaginings all can see black
Listen to the invocation of the devil
From the one you love, think & wish no evil
From beginning to end thinking of love
To be scorned for not doing enough
"Love conquers all", we are told
True! In the days of old
And today's world money speaks
And the flow pace set for all creeks.

Go into the chapel and up the altar of love
Harbouring no thoughts of hiccough
Before the gloom from human nothingness
And the endless quest for this worldliness
Their grips on your world get
For experiencing that dark past, no regret!


## The Death of Darling

My ears drank yesteryears
The sweet melody of Darling without fears
And not long after "he is a nice person"
Came in stead of Darling like a parson

To replace and bury that tenderness
Painting a tableau of death and sadness
When Darling gives way to a nice person
Like the waves for this reason
Smoothly glide and move on
To avoid the mourning robe people put on
For Darling dead here
Is Darling born there
And marked by respect and not scorn
The gravedigger with a nice person adorned
To give the chimera of care
When behind the brain is all ware
Wearing away true love for an illusion
Sparked by some promises of affection;
False love is that on board
And truer love lurks abroad!

That's their word
Yet, the voice tells inward:
"Love and love faithfully
Move and move on freely
When Darling is killed and buried
Spurring ire that leaves man worried…

With the figment of imagination
The drive set in motion
Must be underlined the need
To scurry to the mire such a deed
With just notification
The only justification."

# Forty Years after, No Honey

Good old Spiro never bowls.
Behind his apron mends soles.
He does his soul delight in pleasures
Of yesteryears which today he treasures.
Came I to his shop to mend my shoes
He told me nothing I have to lose
'Coz in Ancient Greece and his of forty years ago
Matrimony came close to nothing of today's show
For all a man needed was that in his pants
No accessories and no extras in the pants
When a man his whiskers stretched were 4 women
At his feet which tides have now turned against men
For their pants must have pockets full
If not stingers will fill their pool
And men forced to swim in it, like it or not
If not they will rot or like a distant dot
Become unseen a few years after with no honey left
In Spiro's case forty years went by before honey left
Questing with keen interest the future for man
Good old Spiro shouted, "My man! My man!
They'll all have to cook and clean the mess for years
They've made and will receive no applause but jeers."
I just agreed for the future is already home
Where my orders I receive from butts seated on foam.

# The Pursuit

Pursuing a thirst quenching trough
I knocked about the world
Carrying with me one word,
Met with an optimist,
Met with a pessimist;
The one in time could see a healer
The latter in him saw a killer
Healer
      Or
           Killer
Killer
      Or
           Healer
What's time got to do with LOVE?

           LOVE is not sick
           And needs no stick
           Held by a healer
           For she rules killer
           Her wave sweeps killer clean
           Leaving the healer lean!

# Questions For Union

What is his/her origin?
Do his/her parents distil gin?
What is his/her profession?
What is his/her level of education?
At which university did he/she earn a degree?
Which don is his/her referee?
What is his/her cast/class?
Is his/her clime rich in gas?
Is he/she liberal or unionist?
Conformist
Traditionalist
Non-conformist
Labour,
Slabour
Conservative
Or Derivative ?
Is he/she Marxist?
Communist or Capitalist?
Dem. or Rep.?
White or blue collar plebe?
What car does he/she drive?
Is he/she of the robe, sword or knife?
What is his/her religion?
Is he/she of this or the foreign legion?
How handsome is he?
How beautiful is she?
How much does he/she make?
Does he/she stool cake?
How much has he/she got in the bank?
Is he/she made of gold or plank?
How many mansions does he/she own?

What does he/she carry as stone?
How much dowry does she bring?
How much bride price does he bring?
Where does he/she live?
Has he/she gone through the sieve?
What national is he/she?
Why will he/she choose me?
What else won't one ask before engagement?
These never ending questions to commitment
Trash that which quest:
Were one to bring the best
The best of all these in readiness
To still everything happiness
Would we readily trade bliss for earthly savings
Earthly things we shall all leave behind cravings?
And I would all asked how much happiness
Both shall know in earnestness
My own question for a lasting union
In which none over one has dominion
Like no form of nationalism better than the other.
For, those questions birth the other,
Which otherness
Kills happiness
And not a murderer I would its birth
And so will I do till my final breath.


## The Flash of Beauty

From the horizon your beauty
Did flash
Hardly
Did one think of a backlash

What a beauty, flashing!
What a beauty lashing and slashing!
The price for drinking you with the eyes
As ice solid will never melt like ice;

You, godly apple,
Juicy and appetising
To all eyes and making them wrestle
Thinking their dreams they were realising

But your flash
Did and does blind
To the reality that a lash or slash
From you will all grind.


## Weak Strength!

Hide not insecurities
Behind firmness
That strength might weakness
Be, leading to casualties.

Be soft with him or her that does love you
And blessings never few will be
And dance you will as a happy bee
And perchance clamped, come will love to your rescue.

# The Infidel Spouse

You go to church
I do not as much
But our thoughts?
One from droughts
Suffer
Proper!

Money,
    Money,
        Money!
Dream,
    Dream,
        Dream!
Will smile bring
Will fame bring
Will bring joy
Will give the children toy!
That's the groom to espouse
You voraciously browse
Crumbling under its weight
Smile, fame, joy and toy still wait
For hate, heartlessness, arrogance
And insolence unveil their fragrance
With my back against your dream
Savouring life by the stream
And aspiring no longer after her
But death to behind leave her
Seeing unfaithful will she still be
And even to money!

Honey!

Honey!
          Honey!
Taste!
     Taste!
          Taste!
Bring sweetness
Kill bitterness
With such hearty drops,
But once past the taste buds…?
Dream or money,
Taste or honey,
Arrogance or sweetness,
Joy or bitterness,
Usher to a desert
Devoid of dessert…!


## All Apostles?

What has a woman before marriage?
The size of a wasp!
What does she become after marriage?
A giant size WASP!

Did the French not say so?
Is there any who is a wasp?
Does any sting more than the giant size WASP
Killing the Red in the field behind the Negro?

Seeing the frail and feeble
Thrown into the wild for standing firm
For all they had was belief and no firm
And seeing not a sting feasible

Then an open arm they gave
And below the belt a blow did receive
Before they could open eyes to no reprieve
That not even the reservations its way did pave

Woman, woman,
Lady, Lady,
Liberty, Liberty
Why do this to Man?

Be him Indian or African, red, yellow, blue, black or white
Be him Buddhist, Christian, Hindu, Muslim, animist or
agnostic
Don't you see in the various creeds something apostolic?
Woman, why not push aside your spite?


## Lady Z

Lady Z, Sing, sing,
Sing and sing

Bowing down to your ladyship,
In Love, of none I dreamt but friendship

Believing: "no poet quakes!

Under the mass of adversity,
He embraces with sagacity."

Our story was this simple
And I won't add it a dimple
Yet, you multiplied your woes

And sent me many, many foes!

My thirst
Does quest:

What of Ogden, the poet
Who of everybody a poet

Makes?

Or did her ladyship for moneys
Trade the universal man of justice?

This I thought her ladyship above
Most especially thinking we were in love

And still a poet, I won't fake
My commitment, your blows I did take!

No more ripple
I won't dribble!

Only wonder if you can swear
As I do of our love its garment wear!

Still will bow to your ladyship
And still of none dream but companionship

Sing, sing, sing to us a song
And asleep we won't see you wrong!

# Platter of Abuse

Counting beads,
Stalling breeds

Serves not just

My cute,
Cute

Suit on libel
On each face
Without pace
Leaving a wrinkle

On a suit
That's my fruit,

To dribble
Like ripple
Sounding
Echoing
Tornadoes with Abuse
On a platter for their use
With icy cold
Callous gold

To be honoured
And honoured

And to face charges
And charges

But from human eyes slays trust

T' hailing them great men!
For crushing the stamen!

Yet, would the platter bury
Or explode with fury

For this act so devilish
To a nation they by day ravish

Against this abuse
Justice should run in for use!


## Yellow Leaf Forever

Old, yellow
With wrinkle
Unseen periwinkle
Yellow
Poor old Africa
Old poor Africa
Looked upon like leaves
Autumn tree leaves
For Fall ready to fall
For the world to glory at a ball
You do in you conceal
A treasure seal
With your yellow
The golden gold yellow
In your entrails buried
Where our diggers have us buried.

Thence draws the light of day
Its ray bringing the light of day
To brighten our lost soul
Treated with the dole.


## Poisonous Heart

The lovely poisonous heart
Beats for no other heart…!
With effusion putting up,
Venom, not blood pumping up
Would scream your best
Interest
Is at heart;
Take your hand and your heart
Would arrest
And send you to rest
And with you resting in peace
In others still would it seek peace`!


## K Joiner

Like the storm Katrina sweeps men off their feet
Her act set them quaking in a feat
And they fall for the last first kiss
Ready to cross the ocean for this bliss.

Joiner
Heart rescuer
Stop not to blow
For it will these hearts deal a blow!

# The Walls of My Love

The concrete walls of my love
Are steel strong gluing my cove
Unflinching to the flame of enmity that burns
But do embrace a fiery passion that turns
Any one hundred and eighty degrees
With or without Degrees
To follow their heart
And on their target land like a dart
To their pounding heart still
Cognisant another heart does theirs steal
For barricaded by these love walls
Not even a shelled volley their love stalls
Stalling the freshness of love
Needing neither perfumes nor a trough
'Coz it is oxygen pure
And does a thirst cure
And like the Spring
Does joy bring.


# The Lion and Attraction

With the Attraction
Of attention
By the beauty of a rose
From its lazing ground, the lion rose
And thought might would
Make him loved in the wood.
Might failed him!
Coercion he embraced to bail him
Forgetting might and intimidation

Words not in Rose's lexicon!

## Tears for Peace and Love

Passions, humans do express in ways different
Some positions totally indifferent
Some in the aquarium, the gold fish
Freedom deprive and others in their plates relish!

From within my soul I caged a bird
A bird I caged from birth
Making it my everything
When the world turn around to nothing!

Chased out of the window is the dove!
And the tears from my eyes sing for Peace and Love
And query what is to this world left, if the poet
His voice loses and sings not his part in the duet?

Let the tears roll down the cheeks
Let them roll to fill all the creeks
With the poet's natural glove
He wears for mankind to find that grove.

Being all poets let's head for the dove
And bring him home, with our heads up above
Up above the mire of blood they would we drowned
In. Poets do ignominy drag down! Down, down, down!

# Dulcet

Like a gentle breeze the music caresses
Human hearts with the softness of fleece
Leaving humans nodding agreeably
Seeing the leaves play the music joyfully
Bringing home the perfumes from lands
Far, far away through which smells to those lands
Transported we are
And thus can see no land is far
For the mind's eye has everything near
And no distant sound away from the ear
And no sweetness of love untasted
Not already tasted
For our everything,
When all is left with nothing
'N by rogues shattered a piece,
Is any dulcet piece.


# The Longing

I went round looking and looking for little miss pretty
The one I saw and thought was, close to home went for pa
money
So, never was any deal done
For her desire would be foregone
For I had no money but affection
Which in turn stood miles from her attention
And all I could was pray money bought her some
                    Now that I know pretty is not about form!
            Welcome miss hideousness if she has a heart
            Not like the gun above pointing at a heart

And with desire money can buy a gun
And same money will never drum the fun:
Affection far from her reflection would
Gently soothe any lost soul in the wood
A dream most will like to have
Than live and die with no laugh


## Love Sake

Hit your chest and look at me as a fool
'Coz on me everyone sits as on a stool
Yet, I thought I'd be your throne
Not knowing you'd have me thrown
But as a fallen man I fear no fall
And laugh at sacks of flesh and bones up tall
In pride and arrogance
Only to fall in trance
Moved by the spirit that humbles
So that no soul ever crumbles;
The spirit in the fallen man
Would never leave any man wan!
Instead of hitting your chest
Priding in what's in your chest,
Hug and embrace a poor fool
Whose spirit makes a good stool
On which wise men will sit
For your kind to smell shit
And leave them in a bind
Simply for they're love blind,
Blind for that's the nature of love
And the love buck's always told off.

Those days when life was up and kicking
I didn't think I would send you to Quiberon
One day I thought I would love find with a run
And it did turn out to be killing
Killing those six years of bliss
Years together I now miss
Ensnared by the flashes of a call
Calls to the heart of darkness appal
And I would you're supreme deity up above
To accept this one time fallen angel with Love
I would rush to the churchyard and lay to rest
The regrets I borne now knowing you're the best
And wishing with life I toiled not playfully;
Any offer from you welcomed heartily.

You did see the thorns and my attention call to them
Like young and foolish Yeats found that a problem
And away peacefully walk knowing not
Next day I would live to your name call out
With you lovingly answering
And for explanations waiting
From a guilt stricken heart with remorse covered
Just dreaming the lost best bet were recovered
With remorse in bloom and willingness to sit upright
After such a great fall I stretch my hand without fright
And you and only you alone know what in the cellar
You have in store for this self-confessed appalling fella
In whose dream your righteousness flinches not an inch
As he now makes strides towards you not thinking lynch.

# Love Hope

There were ten endless years of wait
Which in them did hide hope as bait
Picked and swallowed were blown in a second
Gone is the mansion of such a fecund
Hope
                        Dope
That once turned our desert green
Now turning our green bloom grim
With eternity to say who was right
Not remembering the endless years of fight
With despair it will never come to pass
Which did and our lesson learned out of class
In which the school of life reserves no formula
To grace the lives of those who swear by the kola
Throwing its peelings to tell our future
Or cast a look at our woe like vultures
Tending to a wounded game on the highway
As hope on us preyed in our wait; such they pray!

# Strange

Smooth like beauty herself
The cutting edge herself
Sharp like shark teeth
Won't let love breathe
Breathing to grow
Make rivers flow
To their source
Our dream cause
We follow seeing the shimmer

Of such beauty without flicker
Glimmer and dazzle us
To gathering no moss
Strange! Strange! Strange!
Beauty strange
Things does
Makes worse
Hopes by rulers made bad
Hiding figs from the bats
Ignoring leveller will all level
Six feet underground dug with a shovel.

# Flower Pot Music

Would no one tell the world
Of melodious mused word
Adorning my computer
Singing so sweet potted flower
Music no one hears
Even those with ears
But the eyes on which she strikes the chords
Softly and carefully against odds
The pot the drum
Does the heart plumb
The flower
The drummer
Sending one up the ladder of joy
And up he should go without being coy
Ready to feast the eyes
Like a child sighting rice
Without price weighing on his kind
In a world none has him in mind
Safe flower pot drumming colour
Spurring tears of joy not dolour
Saying why no one hears
'Coz the lot harbours fears.

# Fill Thy Measure Full

True lover, love's triple fool
Keeps love's cup constantly full;

First fool does fall in love
The second takes blind love

Clenching his fist and would die by it
The third fool does everything forfeit

For his or her love to live a dream true or untrue
Minding not he or she chose the right or the wrong crew.

What on earth is worth a triple fool
Who for love does his measure fill full?

Caring less for ancestral squabbles
They would all squander love's true fables

Love's triple fool would avoid such foible
Were they to be taken in for libel!

# Zero!

Away from you, my sweet fleshy lass
To you my thoughts I trust as none has.
So, worry, you need not worry.
My choice for you is our glory.
A point I need not slave to make
For my love for you has no stake.
All I know is O!
A perfect round O!

## Love by the Right Dose

The world has eyes on you as a rose.
But my loving soul sees the right dose
To stall hunger
To beat thunder
To quench great thirst
For you're the first
And the last
I'll not last
Without for any other love
Just little O flying up above
Beating the wings
My heart beating
As they do flap
For you I clap!
When you do hear,
Roads will be clear
By the right dose of love
Consummated by Jove
Sending Bacchus to roam

Embracing O at home
         L
  ve
         tell
                        ye
         I crave
No grave
To kill a rose
With overdose.


## We'll Fly

Numbing the pain
Numbing the brain
True love does
Good beer does
Take closer to heaven or hell
As literature does its bombs shell
Heating and chilling the graves
And will the tomb stone engrave
An honest man and politician
Life is wrought by one magician
Call him Love
Call him Jove
From the tap
Set no trap
Let love flow
Let beer grow
The pain will die
We'll always fly
Painlessly in a dream painted love
In which colour one sees nothing rough

In a beautiful life with grunge removed
Thanks to which creativity we're so moved
Seeing life in a waveless sea sail
And in so good a health, not this frail.


## Voice to My Words

I dream of a voice to make a song
Of these words I have penned for long
Long in waiting for eternity
Which I will love till infinity
To chime the bells that drive hearts from school
And taught us words may be the right tools
Translating emotions with the right voice
That will bring out what's in the mind not noise
To sooth a longing soul to sing longing
Never to end this song that is beginning
To brighten the dawn of this dream day
Whose sharp edgèd sword does all pain slay
Erecting with just words a strong love bond
On both sides of the mountain far beyond
So, every time I stand still like prime time
Contemplating none but my love, no crime
Would be the load sinking me as I stand
With full knowledge mine is no sinking sand
Though the wind from the ocean sweeps my shore
Taking all I know; not my Love for Sure!

# Love Professor Screwed

When your old man said, I was cut for you
And that your choice was mere photo for you
My career goals, I put on hold for you
My back, I turned on family for you
My back, I turned on many friends for you;
Even children I abandoned for you
Having thoughts their mother was none but you
Turning towards you, I have this for you:
Note! I won't fight a man over you
If you miss him much I'll let him have you
As for me, I won't let any fight you
Over me be them Libra girls like you
Lost in dreams men wait twenty years to screw;
No wonder the rest has been about you!

# Sky Kissing Earth

I saw the skies running to the end
Of the earth to kiss her as a friend
Driving a hearse of strange bedfellows
The one on the throne, the other follows
All in the name of life hereafter
For the sake of blood thirsty gods slaughter
Not this hearse now transporting them home
Home bitter home. They would our streets roam!
Painting her red to send us home for peace
Their right to covet the Golden Fleece.

# Love You Forever

Libra boy Aeries girl
Should I say Libra girl?
What happened to "Love you forever?"
That was then. And as of now? Never!
He didn't compel you to believe
So accuse him not he deceives;
You your choices make, so assume them!
Blame it not on his promise. Problem!
The past does charm the future to be
The one that in the past was no bee
Stinging and drumming pain I do chase
Accepting your flaws a passing phase
Frozen in time as you turn your back
From my love and care to prove you lack
Not one to love and care as I do
Your exchanges will get close. He too
Will be by your icy coldness burnt
Then you'll learn not all can bear such brunt
Christ shouldered his cross the bible claims
I shoulder you and still take the blames!
Follow your shadows and set me free!
I will breathe oxygen from the tree
Till I become food for my feeder
And my pen will like a he-goat bleat
Boring songs moving no soldiers feet
You'll see what you've taken for granted
Just as your desire for him granted.

# Hi Stranger! Miss You!

You men and women wearing my shoe make
Know where it pinches; your cries won't be fake!
Politicians grace their speak with sincerity
So do some brides and grooms swear by fidelity
Before you sit up, their exes become strangers
Not long after that they swear by love forever
Sweeping a desert clean of sand before your eyes
With hands leaving chills down the spine, ice
Cold and freezing the desert heat wave
And swear you telling them misbehaved
You can't be missed! You are always home!
Dreaming of being missed? Depart home!
Know peace perfect peace, then they'll the itch
Scratch and tell the world you were the hitch
'Twixt them and their stranger they dearly
Kiss in absentia and dream only
Of their touch as you homely them touch
His homelier touch their vision torch
Bright with promises honey won't come
Close to being sweet when miss become
Real reality not one in studio
Concocted and sung on the radio,
Thing of the past not this day and age
When the Internet plays the backstage
Where no one shall see them in true love
Hi Stranger! Miss you no more! The glove's
Fallen now their turn on the summit
To climax and on our heads drop shit.

# Demon in the Attic

Merry making like festive mice in grain bags
This demon copies rain bringing clouds and brags
Opening these chapters of questions than nuts
Hard to crack for any attempt would drive nuts
The law rules not where his dominion he's made
So, with head and heart aches people are being paid
For neither the polls nor brute force will oust him
And his resolve to skin thin our mansion slim.


# Smells of Death

To some it smells like a rotten rat.
To others? A delicious platter!
They must their own hands use to come by
And I wonder why they do comply.
There I see death dying and leaving
Me alone in the whole world as king
King over those who smell rats
King over those who eat from platters
With turtle soup and venison decorated
In such glittering restaurants with some stars rated
Rejecting all the dirty poor crown of mishaps
No commoner will ever string joy to with harps
As they promise heaven and earth to these poor souls
Waiting and waiting to be guided to the doles
In which they'll have to wait and wait for the drum sound
Marking the end of the show with them homeward bound.

# Love in Pitch Darkness

I fell in love in pitch darkness
My thoughts went straight to love blindness
In which like any frightened kid
Myself I bundled up and hid
By the corner of the dark room
Making pictures of love with broom
Sweeping the darkest part of night
I learnt was that minute of night
Just before the break of any day
So, I dreamt on, waiting for pay
Having loved dearly and patient
In hope break of day was lenient
Hoping and hoping until hope
Come eat this little brain like dope
Pushing the deadliest euphoria
To invade just like diphtheria
Such transparent depths of true love
Consumed by desire from lust's stove.

# Treason Felon

The man down the road pays the price
Yet, his master's dog won't eat rice
In their world where he on the streets
Is the enemy all would beat
With the dog with mastery over
Friendship upheld by the master;
Dog, man's best friend.
Man? Man's worst friend!
Docking himself into a church claiming

Credence at the same time caging
Humanity within the walls of a prison
Void of light, shined with accusations of treason
Not the infant world my nursery,
Nursing friendship not of mystery
To binding men together,
Comes to the table to garner.
Tell me how sweet life would be, were
Both man and master forever
Best friends with both under a roof
With none on the other with hooves
Crushing not only him but his dreams
Of laughter and smiles full; no screams!

## The Face of Beauty

Underneath that heart lies beauty
By a mind upheld and lauded
Translating through an angelic voice
Such values of lofty finds
The values of all such finds
Should never sane minds deter
With envelopes shaped with beauty.
In rags a cheerful heart's pretty!
And will nasty thoughts peter

# She Went to School

She went to school in England
I welcomed her back to land
And was made foreigner at home
What a crush given a coxcomb…!

Jumping from frying pan to the fire,
To ashes burnt and swept into the mire
Coxcomb in a pool of sleeplessness swims
Seeing her drive away with chants she wins

Victory now! Tomorrow, History! Sorrow
Kicks in with qualms lining up in a row
The one wheelchair bound, the other knocked out
This new flash of light turns a playboy out

Then teary river with tears will flow
With pains coxcomb received from the blow
Drummed with privation of consummation
Clamming up emotions once in motion

This leather bag filled with flesh, shit and bones
That leather bag filled with flesh, shit and bones
Most ignore dying and rotting somehow
Just no point chanting dominance with howls.

# Some Desires

Some people would their names in history
Written for their misdeeds, so petty;
They would it read they snatched from that man
That one dream he had in a woman
So lascivious to unwrap herself
In the bed of adultery himself

They come in history not as makers
But would be remembered, dream breakers
With their disease that kills human hopes
With their sweetest tongues that pull the ropes
Noosed round the neck of the beautiful
Beauty outwardly in with shit full

Say the least there is more than physic
Attached to the birth of a lyric
Ludicrously chiming the sad tune
Dealing a deadly blow to the dune
Blown away by the motion now set
Hoping humans will never forget

Further human history does fall short
Of all else and soon become a sport
Most desire for kicks to rile others
With orders from underworld masters
Taken and executed at best
As the only way they can know rest.

# Tamara

Little Mexican girl, when we met that summer
Your crimson red did stick out just like a flower
We fell in love
Madly in love
Led by Jove
To the cove
That's where we came
And without shame;
Doing it in all positions
Caring not in what situation
Falling
Standing
Lying
Spinning
Sitting
Jumping
Flying
Landing
And to the ground
You turned around
In your words: "You know what?"
And I sought after that!
Hearing I'll be father of four
For you and not father for four
Preordained before hand by a wife
Meeting one like you must be my strife;
Failing to heed this, on the way to hell
Am I bound as you must the world tell
From the depths of love where is no doubt
Mothering them you'll forever be proud
And I forever shall know

peace
Which even the ice shall not freeze
Yet, my ears I did block to this day
Harvesting your prophecy as pay,
Fruit of which taste not sweet but bitter

For thinking you desired a litter.


## How Far to Go?

Save her from the grip of madness
Lay her the grounds for happiness
Where the overpowering spell shake
Making her make of icing the cake
Her favourite sport we now witness
In us she sees only weakness
Clearing rocks and thorns afoot mountain
Her aim being the top of the mountain
That is how far she would go
Impressing us we are slow.


## Lullaby for Love

I got up at one end of this world
And would have happily screamed: dear Lord!
When my thoughts in haste to my love dashed
To learn she was asleep; she'd just crashed!
Yet, love told me to drown my love with love
In a sea of sweet dreams painted all love
As my muse kept alive my ears
With lullaby I would she hears

And soothes her panting heart
Knowing love throws no dart.

## Before the Courts

Here I come before the Bar!
I left the place where you are
Leaving behind me, with you, my heart
And with me I took you in my heart
And as I journey along
We now both quest: for how long?
We know not!
It drives nuts!
Love courts charge me guilty; guilty for leaving
Yet, make known why I'm nailed to pay for leaving
When you have my heart!
I have you at heart!
Love this is
Without fleas!
If not bring the crucifix
And leave lovebirds in a fix!

## Our Separate Ways

I have seen parting
I have parted
Not departed
Still I see parting
Done by the books,
Oh, no, by crooks
Whose souls delight

In quenching light
That once showed the way
With hopes as sole ray!
By the books or a crook,
At the end, get off hooks
And freedom breathe wholly whole!
Trash her delight in a hole!


## The Second Christening

The names my parents gave me
All meant everything for me
But the day Love called me Farai,
I jumped with fright and was all shy
Learning this old Shauna word
My soul created a new world
One on which happiness on his throne
Had crushed sadness with disgust and thrown
In a land of horny sweet dreams
Where human kindness flood the streams
And sweep clean all inanity
That has a grip on our city.


## Walk the walk

True love walking in
A big bag bringing
With meaning full, strong like lion
Does throw out chameleon
Siphoning grasses' colour
Leaving pure hearts with pallor

Now come and stay
We will dance and play
In this arena with no room
For gloom feigned love to be the bloom;
Green eyed monsters loudly hailed
Thanks to whose kindness we had wailed
Wishing the wailers weren't thieves
Leaving our wail the sound of leaves


## Run for Love

Struck by stroke
One of luck
I hope it turns
Not the grave nigh
With hellish beauty
Bringing death forthwith
A drunk so like dope
Seeking heavy pay
From those who would dare
To play with a drum
One to still users
Leaving dope all wan
And mad with madness
To remand brigands
Guiding the wheel helm
To benumb feelings
Leaving big scars too
Unjust to our beings
Where human hearts stood
Dreaming love out there,
Out there, there is love

To come with no pout;
Much so, without spite
And having no crutch
Love, this is true love
Soaring above Jove
Of material void
By itself enough
Calling neither stroke
Nor bringing falling
Close to fallen blinds
Who'd seen love as rose
Until by stroke struck
To their measure fill
Full with questioning
And thoughtlessness full
Crowding wounded hearts
Tearing and bleeding
Tears and blood unseen
By all drowned in fears
Those for ignoring
Love should by the dose
Be administered
If not like a bee
Sting comes that which kills
Joys of calm loving
That of qualms dreamt not
It would harbour darts
Planted by hatred
To true love wicked
Showing callousness
To stop love flowing
In the direction
The river within

Mapped as the one course
Never to be sapped.

## Seeing on 20th, Meeting on 21st

You tell me you're Patience
Your love does sing silence
Only heard from within
And followed without being
Thomas tied to things seen!
My pure love shan't be sin.
But tongues shall wag and wag
Your head up, you shall brag
And shall in the mud drag
This world's dirty filled bag
Dirty bag filled with slur
Stating after the fur
You had jumped for tanning
All they need for slaying
Loveliness void of stain
And enjoyed free of pain
Love of pain free must be
Ours savoured like honey;
One you are! So sweet, sweet
That you start hearts' drumbeat
To intone Love's music
To sooth a heart that's sick.

# Strong Rock Solid Love

My word my bond with you here will stay
Far from the love that did rot away
For you so love me that I won't doubt
And if I did so, I won't call out
As I do by the day and by night
Showing you the love that's yours by right.

Here I sit and here I wait, you in mind
Being the special find by mankind
Sought after in that love threadbare world
In which like the serpent hatred curled
Around in wait for the innocent
In order to prey on sentiments

Where you are, there I am on my marks
Ready to take you home with no barks
For those dogs willing to still our move
To push our love right atop the roof
Shading new meaning to the word love
With sound knowledge of peace brought by dove

Here we are, love we know that will stay
With no one able to make her sway
From this gleeful glide on these smooth rails
Leading home a love that blazes trails
For dreamers who slain their dreams way back
With no thoughts someday it will come back.

Now we know what to keep that we've found
Which is what in love will keep us bound
Together loving and respecting

Each other with just no misgiving
But thanks giving to the light that lights
Love's path on which we tread without plights.

Count the lines; know the span it'll survive
In the eyes of men striding in life
All clad in abjection fanning flames
Heating up the air for baseless claims
Claims that in our union has no grounds
Where our rock solid love's ever sound.


## Sheila is All

Just when I was about to give all up
I saw sincerity marked on love's face
By Sheila; she was patient with grace
That off my feet knocked and swept me to drop

Head over heels as if by a spell doomed
To this life of happiness as a groom
With honey textured soul in readiness
To cast away that life of moodiness!

With such love am I graced to embrace her
With my glance at her, looking no further
As the bells resound with marital bliss
Leaving me nor any room for a bliss

Tell me why the world I shouldn't give up
For one so dear lifting me to the top
In form and in spirit full with pleasure
Caressing the heart, knowing no measure.

The strength of love bonds with understanding
Giving our show to the world, astounding
And hoping not in history such would be
You the bee that produces sweet honey

And who said honey was sweet? You're sweeter!
You make the bitterness in life slumber
Like one who has come and come till he can't
Embrace and understand jack by Kant.

But once into your bee hive with honey
Full, the genius in him would spite money
And would start digging in nature, pleasure
As would any hunter hunt his treasure.

My Sheila had laid patiently in wait
And such treasures as Sheilas are no bait
But babes to be cherished and lavished well
With love that runs deep, the like of my well!


## Our Growing Love

As my love for you grows, so shall their throat swell
And so shall they a past brew for you to smell
Frustrated more and more like a cat's tail shall
Their tongues begin to wag and wag; dying fall
Sets foot in announcing bleak scary winter
That like the 1812 General will hamper
This great love growing from a seed so minute
As the baobab's that grows and makes men mute;
Mute they shall succumb when all else shall have failed
But for our steel strong love for which we'll be hailed!

# What D.... does!

Darling would teach me how to sing
She is the only song I sing,
The only song to which I listen
The only book I have written
The only book I am reading
In her sleep I hear her snoring
Her snoring, the music of love
Flying high above like great Jove
Whose fart is pure air freshener
And spit? Thirst quenching water!
With sweat in which I bathe by night
Dreaming not in this sleep of blight
But her smile the key to my heart
Letting my wings flap like a bat's.

# The sound of Reality

Reality sounds like a dream
Not the one in which we scream
But in it do freely swam
And stay in without a squirm
Such dreams people find too hard
To swallow were one not a bard.
Lauding this sound reality
Most don't dream of in history

# To You I Sing

I love this song
To you I sing
This old folk song
Each lip would sing
With fewer feet to it
Dancing the tune with it
Rhyming just with the ring
That blinds to the jingling
Bell bringing to minds flings
That leave nothing but stings
Here I stand to declare
A heart so pure and clear
That would sing, "I love you"
Those never sang to you
But dreamt to take your hand
With promises a band
Would to the altar lead
Your heart void of misdeed
That fills their empty vows
To you as their milk cows;
Cow you are not but Love
That projects me above
Rulers, straight and erect
Which I check as correct
Indeed for you're spotless
Covered with worthiness
To you I sing
Joy it shall bring!

# I Refuse

Donne sang a song to go catch a falling star
Targeting the woman when man is that star.
How often have men faltered undeterred
In life and have stood up with wives battered?

I won't catch a star, rising or falling
But would men and women in love singing
From morning till dawn, from twilight till dusk
Leaving the smoothness of elephant tusks,

This glittering ivory painted a heart dark
To reducing our voices with its bark
Which to this day we've been up to silence
With fervent zeal exhibiting patience.

# Give the World

Give the world the wherewithal
To think one man one knife dull
With nothing I would the world tell
One man many wives is real hell

‡
††
卌
††††

And if womankind finds in
One hunter one spear boring,
It should learn many spears through hearts
Will simply fly to split the hearts.

††††
†††
††
†

# Dreams Die Not

When dreams mature, they cease to be dreams.
When streams dry up they cease to be streams.
One dream I had, I thought would bear fruits
Let my stream flow into its conduits
Without dam built but quickly emptied
To leaving my dream in stream buried.
But how wonderful dreams do not die
Like the hungry poor deprived of pie!
And buried 'live won't be dreams that live
To be killed only by disbelief
We need kill to give the figment life
Leaving every tongue saying hi-five!


# Two Months After

On my way out of America
None could've convinced me two months after
Solace I'd have found in my woman
For whom in love I fell without qualms

Thinking not of faults for you are mine
With whom I would for sure dine and wine
To gladden my one time cheerless heart
Heartlessness pinned to sniff stinking fart
Such refusing to be a herald
To defend your name's worth must get out
And not in sheepskin come to get you
Now that as Queen you won't smell his pooh!

My nose for years past did all in hope

The wind shall turn such mindset like dope
To this euphoria brought by true love
In which head over hills we're not rough

Yet, like the wind your love my world rocks
With knowledge with pride, to swell like frogs
Challenging none would ever flatten
Them for with true love they are fattened

My woman, yours as a name sits well
With all the virtues that love would spell
And read for weary hearts to have ears,
Hear and shatter nightmares that bring fears

Where with you, courage is born and bred
Hand in gloves with love growing in strength
To dig a grave for that moroseness
Whose life had been to chase happiness

This wish in big baskets you bring forth
And for this your name grows all it's worth
Playing in any man, live music!
This therapy does cure every sick!

# That We Won't Take

We've all loved the wind to come wipe our tears
And bring the change so much fought by their fears
That did build a wall, a wall to stop change
Breathing this life in which none knows revenge;

Payback in its plate served cold, is frozen
And this tranquillity we know sings Zen!
No more cries, no more tears! Just our delight!
In which world, our burden, they had thought light!

Light we refused to take the shit from them
That thought they will win by breaking our stem
Yet, our plight had its roots safe in the fight
We bravely fought to make our future bright

And would the children we loved to beget
Live a life full and fair with no regret
The sharp tips of our pens dug deep such graves
And refused we were not meant to be slaves!

# Blurred Vision

Thoughts of my love clamping up
Drive home a question: what's up?
The air we breathe was for long pure.
This clamping worsens things anew!

Thus, naively, I was schooled to see
A problem shared, one lost at sea
When unshared would create a great rift
That would set all pure love adrift.

Knowing this, I would my best do
Hoping my love did do hers too.
Then and then we shall gracefully
Sail ever after happily.

In this, the world would read black art
Not understood for they're not smart;
Hiding hearts' foliage to love's light,
The greatest cure to all hearts' plight!

Problems abound, love conquers all
With no need to receive a call
From Jimmy Little's telephone
That has been a hard to chew bone.

# Praise for These Poems

The 101 poems in this stunning collection are noted for their lushness of language and simplicity of style as they explore a wide range of emotions while embodying the fearless passion and spirited wit of a poet to whom like Pablo Neruda, words are fun. As you mingle effortlessly through the pages, you will discover that this collection bears the best poetry for new love or old love; requited or unrequited love; fulfilled or unfulfilled love; in fact, any love for as is underscored in the concluding verse of the "The Musical Hand," "Loving infinitely as we do is nothing but wisdom for nothing other than wisdom is infinite!". Why not make this a Veracious Admirable Loveable Valentine present.

Festus Fru Ndeh, Associate Professor of Postcolonial and Theoretical Literatures, Troy University, USA.

Bill offers in his poetic practice true structural complexity, highly verbal with mastery of literary devices and symbolic representation, while at the same time showing himself capable of Blakean epigrammatic terseness... as in 'Val (Veracious, Admirable, Loveable)'. This love poem is of impressive simplicity and yet gains great power on that account. The 101 Love poems in *Sing Love 101* are simple but with great POWER on that account.

Michael Meehan (Academic, Writer and Critic)

*Sing Love 101* as a collection is a billicious gourmet platter with 101 love poems in which this wordsmith worth his words has brought together the good, the bad and the ugly of human love experiences. The poems are glossed with the simplicity of a sweet gentle breeze that caresses the heart of the reader like one blowing across his childhood rice fields in the summer. They remind the reader that True Love supersedes the rage and fury that any disappointment in love can generate. It is in this vain that the poet highlights "Love" as "the Dream" none should let die. In "Dreams Die not" he writes:

But how wonderful dreams do not die
Like the hungry poor deprived of pie!
And buried 'live won't be dreams that live
To be killed only by disbelief
We need kill to give the figment life
Leaving every tongue saying hi-five!

The last two lines of the quotes exhort the reader to kill "disbelief" and give life to dreams (Love). With this done every tongue would say "hi-five". A basic lesson in Love echoing the title *Sing Love 101*. This is an enriching and compelling volume to read.